VEGETABLES

Are Good For You!

by
Gloria Koster

PEBBLE
a capstone imprint

Published by Pebble, an imprint of Capstone.
1710 Roe Crest Drive,
North Mankato, Minnesota 56003
capstonepub.com

Library of Congress Cataloging-in-Publication Data is available on the Library of Congress website.

ISBN: 9781666351286 (hardcover)
ISBN: 9781666351347 (paperback)
ISBN: 9781666351408 (ebook PDF)

Summary: Asparagus, carrots, and garlic . . . What do these foods from the vegetable group have in common? They're all healthy! Explore where vegetables come from, what nutrition they provide, and how they help form a healthy diet.

Editorial Credits
Editor: Donald Lemke; Designer: Tracy Davies; Media Researcher: Julie De Adder; Production Specialist: Katy LaVigne

Image Credits
Getty Images: aluxum, 9, Blend Images–JGI/Jamie Grill, 14, Don Mason, 8, Image Source, 26, Westend61, 5, Yellow Dog Productions, 15; Shutterstock: Aleksandra Suzi, 12, Astarina (veggie doodles), cover and throughout, BearFotos, 20, Creativa Images, 28, Dani Vincek, 7, Diyana Dimitrova, 4, Drazen Zigic, 27, Elena Masiutkina, 17, FamStudio, 13, fizkes, 23, Iraida Bearlala (background), cover and throughout, Ivana Lalicki, 25, Monkey Business Images, 29, petatape, 18, Pressmaster, 19, RAndrei, cover (radish), Rasica, 16, Tada Images, 21, TinnaPong, cover (front), Viktor Kochetkov, 22, Volodymyr Shulevskyy, 6, yurakrasil, 24; USDA: 11

All internet sites appearing in back matter were available and accurate when this book was sent to press.

TABLE OF CONTENTS

Words in **bold** are defined in the glossary.

EAT YOUR VEGGIES

"Eat your veggies!" Why do people say that? Because vegetables are important for good health. They also taste good.

Bake sweet potatoes with butter and brown sugar. Fry cauliflower and top it with cheese. Grill veggies for an outdoor picnic. There are so many ways to eat vegetables!

Vegetables are very colorful!
In fact, veggies come in a whole
rainbow of colors.

Broccoli and asparagus are green. Some radishes are red. Carrots are often orange.

Some beets can be yellow. Potatoes, garlic, and turnips are often white. Some types of cabbages and onions are purple.

People often put vegetables into two groups: **starchy** vegetables and non-starchy vegetables. Both groups have healthy foods.

Starchy vegetables include potatoes and carrots. These veggies have a lot of **carbohydrates**. They give you a quick boost of energy.

Broccoli, cabbage, and spinach are non-starchy vegetables. These veggies are packed full of **nutrients**.

WHY ARE VEGETABLES IMPORTANT?

MyPlate is a guide for healthy meals. Half your plate should have fruits and vegetables. Half should have grains and **protein** foods. A small glass of **dairy** is on the side.

Why are vegetables one of the largest parts? Because veggies are packed with **vitamins** and minerals to keep you healthy!

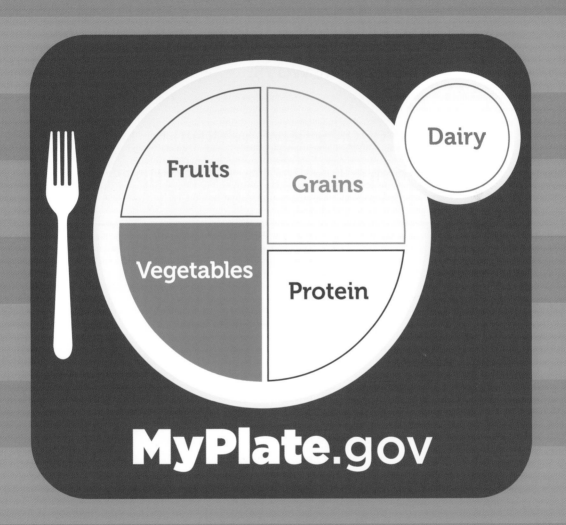

MyPlate.gov

Vegetables have many types of vitamins. Different vitamins help your body in different ways.

Green veggies have vitamin K. This vitamin helps heal cuts and scrapes.

broccoli

carrots

    Lettuce, broccoli, and kale are high in vitamin C. This vitamin helps keep you from getting sick. It also helps your skin stay healthy.

    Sweet potatoes and carrots have vitamin A. Other orange veggies do too. This vitamin keeps your **organs** working well.

Vegetables contain many minerals. Calcium is good for bones. It is good for teeth too.

Potassium is good for muscles. Some types of lettuce have a lot of it. Spinach and broccoli have iron to help you grow.

Veggies also have **fiber**. Fiber is the rough part of food that your body can't break down, or **digest**. Fiber also makes you feel full.

Green beans have a lot of fiber.

HOW VEGETABLES GROW

Vegetables come from different parts of plants. Some veggies are the leaves. Some are stems. Others are the roots of plants.

Red potatoes are root vegetables.

Carrots, radishes, and potatoes grow underground. They are called root vegetables.

Broccoli is the stem and flowers of a plant. Lettuce and kale are leaves.

Vegetables grow in many places around the world. Eggplants, peppers, and yams like hot, rainy weather.

peppers

Another warm-weather vegetable is yuca. It is eaten around the world. Yuca tastes like a potato.

cabbage field

Some vegetables do not like heat.

Turnips and cabbage like cooler temps.

Peas like cooler weather too.

Where do we find all these veggies? Many people grow vegetables in their gardens. Others buy them at a farmer's market. Some get veggies at the grocery store.

vegetable garden

Supermarkets sell fresh vegetables. They also sell frozen vegetables. Some veggies are canned. Some are dried.

Just remember, fresh vegetables are often the healthiest!

EATING MORE VEGETABLES

Vegetarians don't eat meat. They don't eat chicken, beef, or fish. **Vegans** avoid all products made from animals. They don't drink milk or eat eggs either.

Vegetarians and vegans eat only plants for many reasons. Some think it's healthier. Some think it's the right way to live.

Eating less meat and more veggies is good for our planet too.

thali

India is a country with many vegetarians. Thali is an Indian dish. Small bowls are filled with grains and vegetables. They are placed on a large plate.

Falafel and hummus are made from chickpeas. These yummy foods come from the Middle East.

Have you tried bok choy? How about bamboo shoots? These vegetables are common in parts of Asia.

bok choy

Go grocery shopping with a grown-up. Look at the food labels and packaging. Find your favorite vegetables!

When you get home, always wash your fresh vegetables. This removes dirt and sand. It gets rid of chemicals sometimes used to help crops grow.

Then help in the kitchen. Add veggies to soups. Put them in smoothies. Make a rainbow-colored salad.

Skip the chips! Veggies make great snacks too. They have fiber and water. You feel less hungry between meals.

Along with exercise, vegetables will help keep you healthy and strong!

GLOSSARY

carbohydrate (kar-boh-HYE-drate)—a substance found in some foods that gives people energy

dairy (DAIR-ee)—products made with milk

digest (dye-JEST)—the process of breaking down foods in the stomach and organs, so it can be used in the body

falafel (fuh-LAH-fuhl)—a seasoned mix of ground vegetables formed into balls and fried

fiber (FYE-bur)—a part of foods, such as fruits and vegetables, that helps foods move through the intestines

nutrient (NOO-tree-uhnt)—a part of food that is needed for growth and health

organ (OR-guhn)—a part of the body that does a particular job; the heart, liver, and lungs are organs

potassium (puh-TASS-ee-uhm)—a soft metal found in some food that is important for good health

protein (PRO-teen)—one type of nutrient found in food

starchy (STAR-chee)—containing a type of carbohydrate

vegan (VEE-guhn)—a person who does not eat food or use products that come from animals

vegetarian (vej-uh-TER-ee-uhn)—a person who does not eat meat

vitamin (VI-tuh-min)—a nutrient in food that works along with minerals to keep us healthy

READ MORE

Schuh, Mari. *Food Is Fuel.* North Mankato, MN: Capstone, 2020.

Schwartz, Heather E. *Cookie Monster's Foodie Truck: A Sesame Street Celebration of Food.* Minneapolis: Lerner Publications, 2020.

Webster, Christy. *Follow That Food!* New York: Random House, 2021.

INTERNET SITES

Harvard School of Public Health: "The Nutrition Source" hsph.harvard.edu/nutritionsource/what-should-you-eat/vegetables-and-fruits

Healthy Kids Association: "Vegetables" healthy-kids.com.au/food-nutrition/5-food-groups/vegetables

USDA Center for Nutrition: "Kid-Friendly Veggies and Fruits" chfs.ky.gov/agencies/dph/dmch/nsb/Documents/KidFriendlyVeggiesandFruits.pdf

USDA MyPlate: "Vegetables" myplate.gov/eat-healthy/vegetables

INDEX

ABOUT THE AUTHOR

A public and school librarian, Gloria Koster belongs to the Children's Book Committee of Bank Street College of Education. She enjoys both city and country life, dividing her time between Manhattan and the small town of Pound Ridge, New York. Gloria has three adult children and a bunch of energetic grandkids.